MW01153037

The Giant Book of

Christmas Sheet Music For Piano

55 Top-Requested Christmas Songs for Piano Easy Piano Songbook for Begginers

Copyright © 2023

All rights reserved. No part of this publication may be reproduced, stored in a retrieval system, or transmitted in any form or by any means whatsoever without the prior written permission of the publisher, except for brief quotations in critical reviews or articles.

TABLE OF CONTENTS

12 DAYS OF CHRISTMAS

On the first day of Christmas my true love gave to me, a partridge in a pear tree. On the

second day of Christmas my true love gave to me, two turtle doves, and a partridge in a pear

tree. On the third day of Christmas my true love gave to me, three French hens,

two tur-tle doves, and a partridge in a pear tree. On the fourth day of Christmas my

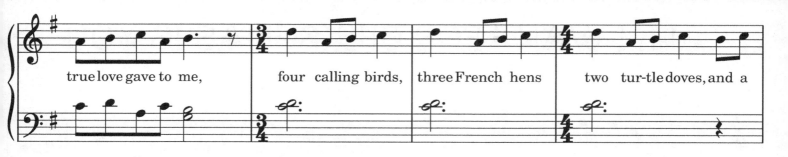

true love gave to me,   four calling birds,   three French hens   two tur-tle doves, and a

par-tridge   in a pear   tree.   On the   fifth day of Christmas my   true love gave to me,

five   gold - en   rings!   Four   calling birds,   three French hens,

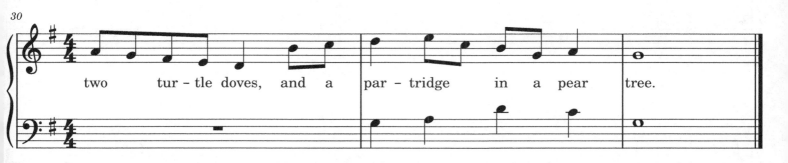

two   tur - tle doves,   and a   par - tridge   in a pear   tree.

ALL I WANT FOR CHRISTMAS IS YOU

♩ = 150

I don't want a lot for Christmas There is just one

thing I need   I don't care a - bout the   presents   un-derneath the   Christmas tree

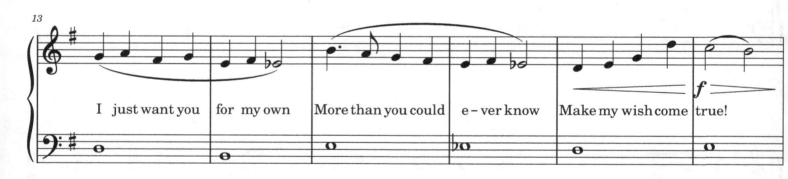

I just want you   for my own   More than you could   e - ver know   Make my wish come   true!

All   I   want   for   Christ - mas   you!

ANGELS WE HAVE HEARD ON HIGH

An - gels   we have heard on high,
Shepherds, why this ju - bi-lee?

Sweet - ly singing   o'er the plains.
Why your joy-ous starins pro-long?

And the mountains
What the glad-some

in   re-ply.
tid - ings be.

E - cho-ing their
Which in-spire your

joy - ous strains.
heaven - ly   song?

"Glo____

____ ri - a.   In ex-cel-sis De - o.   Glo____

____ ri - a.   In ex - cel -sis De____ o."

7

AULD LANG SYNE

AVE MARIA

AWAY IN A MANGER

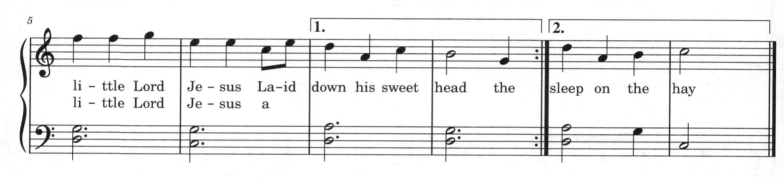

CHRISTMAS TIME IS HERE

BELIEVE (THE POLAR EXPRESS)

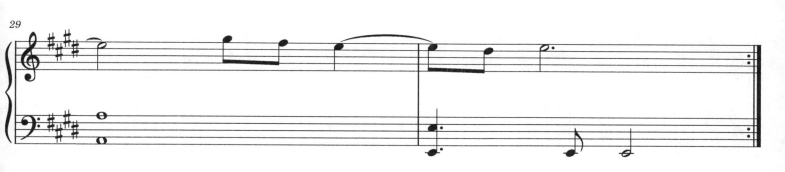

CAROL OF THE BELLS

DECK THE HALL (FA LA LA LA)

FELIZ NAVIDAD

Fe-liz Na-vi - dad   Fe-liz Navi - dad   Fe-liz Na-vi - dad, prospe-ro

a-ño y fe-li - ci - dad   I wanna wish you a   merry-Christmas   I wanna wish you a

mer - ry Christmas   I wanna wish you a   mer - ry Christmas From the   bottom of my

heart___

FROSTY THE SNOWMAN

Fros - ty the snowman was a jol - ly hap-py soul, with a corn-cob pipe and a
Fros - ty the snowman is a fai - ry tale they say, he was made of snow but the

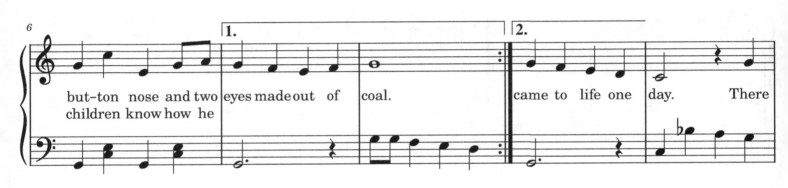

1.
but-ton nose and two eyes made out of coal.
children know how he

2.
came to life one day. There

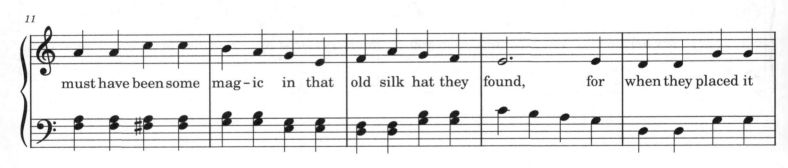

must have been some mag - ic in that old silk hat they found, for when they placed it

on his head he be-gan to dance a - round! Fros - ty the snowman had to hurry on his

way but he waved good-bye saying "Don't you cry, I'll be back a-gain some day." —

Thum pe- ty thump thump thumpe - ty thump thump look at old Fros - ty go,

Thumpe - ty thump thump thumpe - ty thump thump ov - er the hills of snow!

GO, TELL IT ON THE MOUNTAIN

Go tell it on the mount ain, O-ver the hills and ev-ery-where Go, tell it on the

mount-ain that Je-sus Christ is born.

1. While shepherds kept their watch-ing O'er
2. The shepherds feared and trem-bled, When
3. Down in a low-ly man-ger The

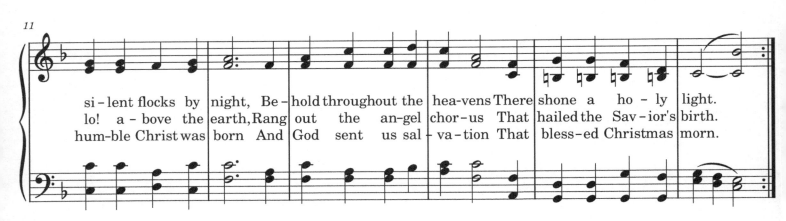

si-lent flocks by night, Be-hold throughout the hea-vens There shone a ho-ly light.
lo! a-bove the earth, Rang out the an-gel chor-us That hailed the Sav-ior's birth.
hum-ble Christ was born And God sent us sal-va-tion That bless-ed Christmas morn.

GOD REST YE MERRY GENTLEMEN

GOOD KING WENCESLAS

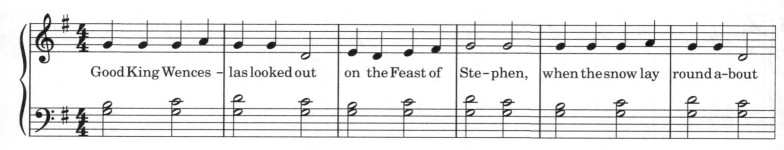

Good King Wences - las looked out on the Feast of Ste - phen, when the snow lay round a-bout

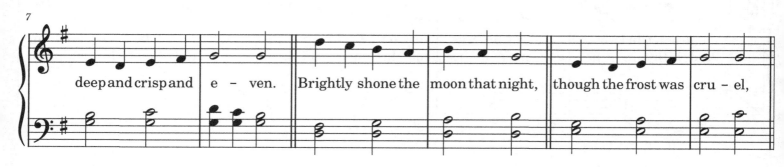

deep and crisp and e - ven. Brightly shone the moon that night, though the frost was cru - el,

when a poor man came in sight gath-'ring win-ter's fu - el.

HARK! THE HERALD ANGELS SING

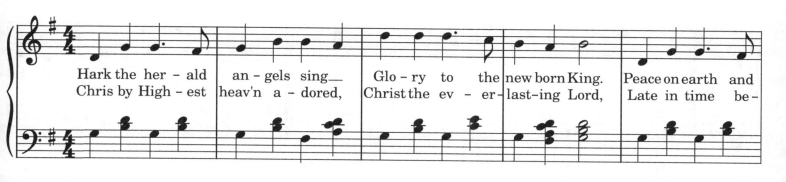

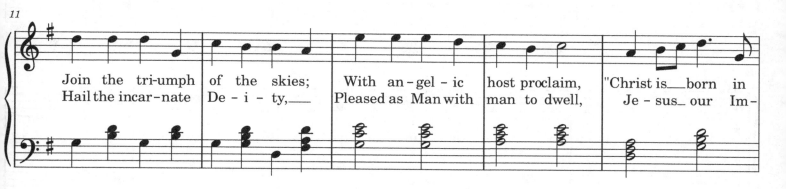

HAPPY NEW YEAR

No more cham pagne and the fi re works are through Here we are me and you feel ing lost and feel ing blue It's the end of the par ty and the mor ning seems so grey so un like yes ter day Now is time for us to say

HAPPY NEW YEAR HAPPY NEW YEAR May we all
YEAR HAPPY NEW YEAR May we all

have a vi sion now and then of the world where ev ry neigh bor is a
have our hopes our wills to try if we don't we might as well lay down and

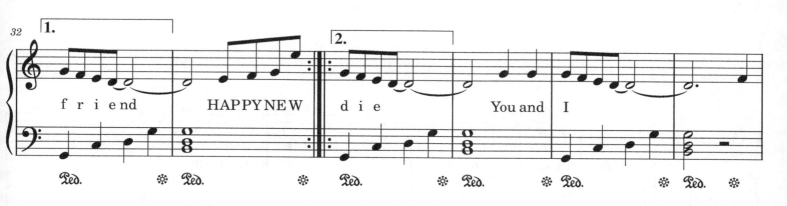

1. friend HAPPY NEW

2. die You and I

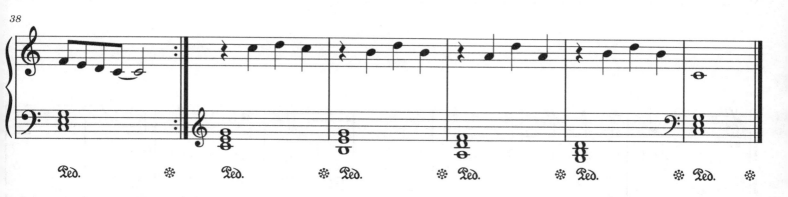

HAPPY XMAS (WAR IS OVER)

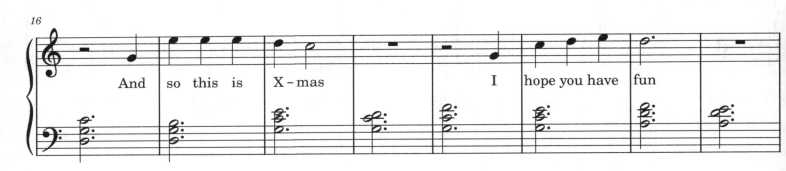

A ver-y merry X-mas and a hap-py new year

Let's hope it's a good one with-out an-y fear

sim.

rit.

HAVE YOURSELF A MERRY LITTLE CHRISTMAS

Have Yourself a merry little Christmas; Let your heart be light From now on our

troubles will be out of sight. Have Yourself a merry little Christmas;

Make the yuletide gay. From now on our troubles will be miles a - way

Here we are as in olden days, Happy golden days of yore; Faithful friends who are

dear to us gather near to us   once more.   Through the years we   all will be togeth-er

If the fates al – llow   Hang a shining star upon the highest   bough

And have yourself a   merry lit-tle Christmas   now.

HOLLY JOLLY CHRISTMAS

♩ = 130 **Swing**

Have a hol - ly jol - ly Christ-mas it's the best time of the year

I don't know if there'll be snow but have a cup of cheer Have a

hol - ly jol - ly Christ-mas and when you walk down the street

Say hel - lo to friends you know and ev - 'ry - one you meet

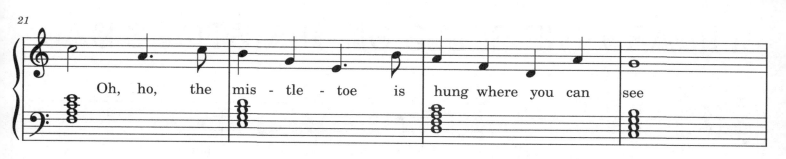

Oh, ho, the mis - tle - toe is hung where you can see

Some - bo - dy waits for you kiss her once for me Have a

hol - ly jol - ly Christ-mas and in case you did'nt hear

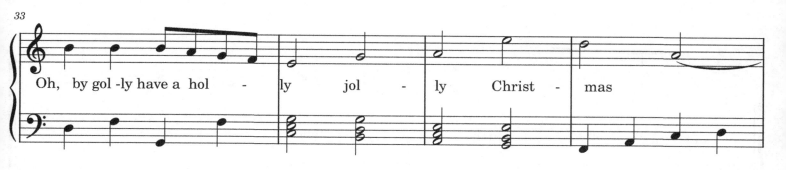

Oh, by gol -ly have a hol - ly jol - ly Christ - mas

this year

I HEARD THE BELLS ON CHRISTMAS DAY

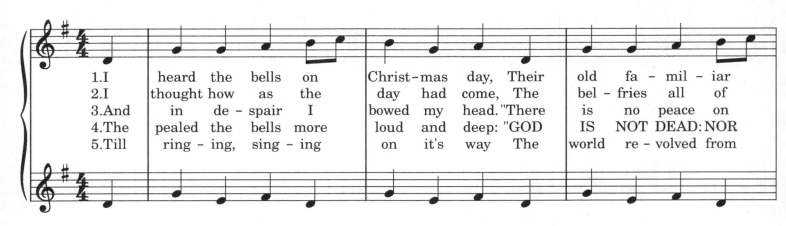

1.I heard the bells on Christ-mas day, Their old fa - mil - iar
2.I thought how as the day had come, The bel - fries all of
3.And in de - spair I bowed my head. "There is no peace on
4.The pealed the bells more loud and deep: "GOD IS NOT DEAD: NOR
5.Till ring - ing, sing - ing on it's way The world re - volved from

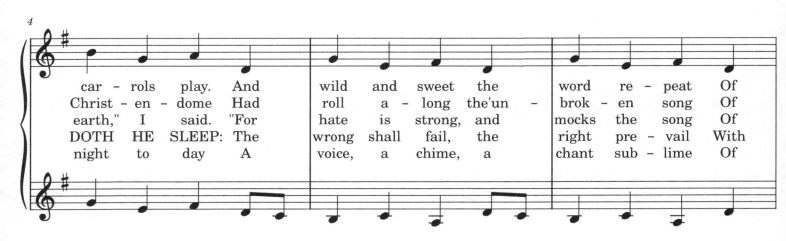

car - rols play. And wild and sweet the word re - peat Of
Christ - en - dome Had roll a - long the'un - brok - en song Of
earth," I said. "For hate is strong, and mocks the song Of
DOTH HE SLEEP: The wrong shall fail, the right pre - vail With
night to day A voice, a chime, a chant sub - lime Of

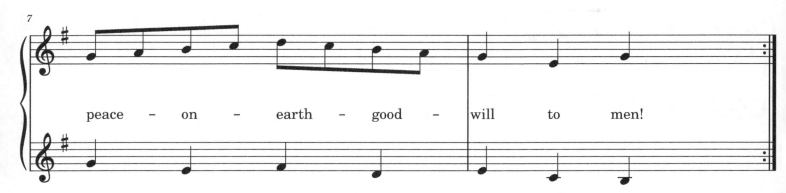

peace - on - earth - good - will to men!

32

I SAW THREE SHIPS

And what was in those ships all three,
On Christmas day, on Christmas day?
And what was in those ships all three,
On Christmas day in the morning?

Our saviour Christ and his lady,
On Christmas day, on Christmas day.
Our saviour Christ and his lady,
On Christmas day in the morning.

Pray whither sailed those ships all three,
On Christmas day, on Christmas day?
Pray whither sailed those ships all three,
On Christmas day in the morning?

Oh, they sailed to Bethlehem,
On Christmas day, on Christmas day.
Oh, they sailed to Bethlehem,
On Christmas day in the morning.

And all the bells on earth shall ring,
On Christmas day, on Christmas day.
And all the bells on earth shall ring,
On Christmas day in the morning.

And all the angels in heaven shall sing,
On Christmas day, on Christmas day.
And all the angels in heaven shall sing,
On Christmas day in the morning.

And all the souls on earth shall sing,
On Christmas day, on Christmas day.
And all the souls on earth shall sing,
On Christmas day in the morning.

Then let us all rejoice amain,
On Christmas day, on Christmas day.
Then let us all rejoice amain,
On Christmas day in the morning.

I SAW MOMMY KISSING SANTA CLAUS

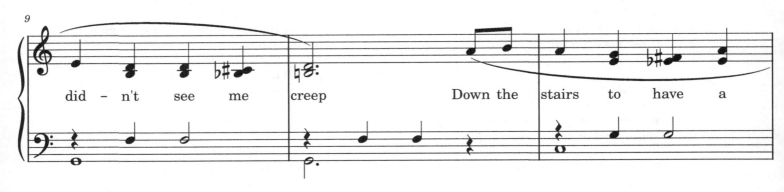

bed-room fast a-sleep. Then I saw Mom-my tick-le

a tempo

San - ta Claus Un-der-neath his beard so snow-y

white; Oh, what a laugh it would have

been if Dad-dy had on-ly seen Mom-my

kiss-ing San - ta Claus last night.

IT'S BEGINNING TO LOOK A LOT LIKE CHRISTMAS

It's be - ginning to look a lot like Christmas   Every where you go

Take a look at the five and ten   Glistening once a-gain, with can-dy canes and

sil-ver lanes that grow   It's be-ginning to look a lot like Christmas

Toys in e-very store   But the prettiest sight to see is the ho-lly that will

IT'S THE MOST WONDERFUL TIME OF THE YEAR

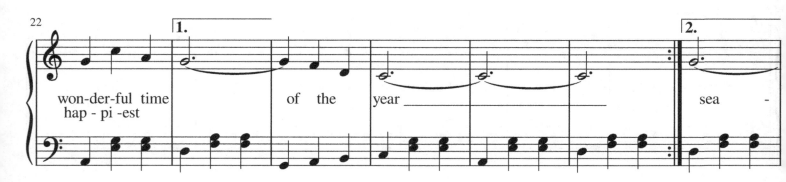

son of all ... There'll be par-ties for hos-ting marsh-

-mel-lows for toas-ting and car-o-ling out in the snow There'll be sca-ry ghost

sto-ries and tales of the glo-ries of Christ-mas-es long long a - go

3.

time ____ the most won-der-ful time It's the most

won-der-ful time of the year ____

Ritardando . . . .

IT CAME UPON THE MIDNIGHT CLEAR

It Came up-on the mid-night clear, that glo-ri-ous song of

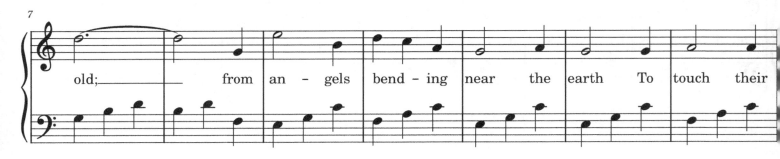

old; from an-gels bend-ing near the earth To touch their

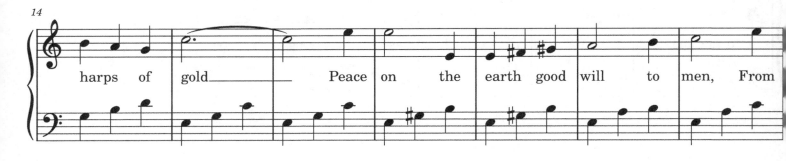

harps of gold Peace on the earth good will to men, From

heaven's all gra-cious King The World in Sol-emn still-ness

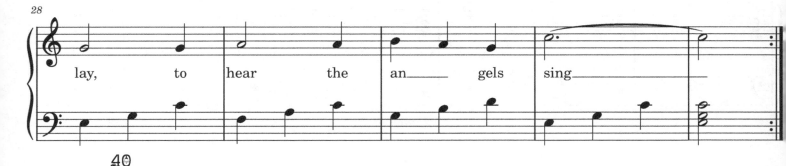

lay, to hear the an-gels sing

JESU, JOY OF MAN'S DESIRING

rall. poco a poco last time through

JINGLE BELL ROCK

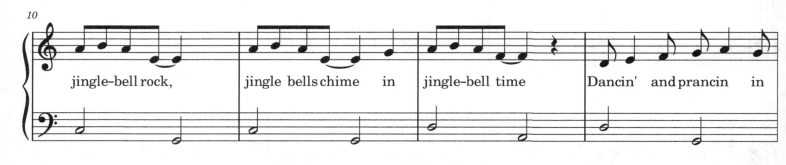

JINGLE BELLS

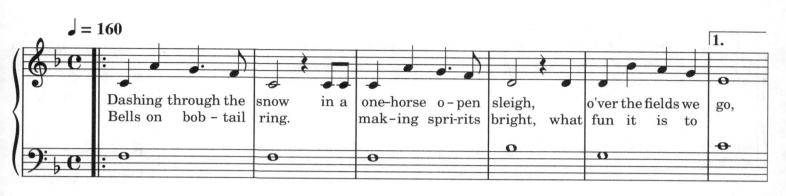

Dashing through the snow in a one-horse o-pen sleigh,
o'ver the fields we go,

Bells on bob - tail ring. mak-ing spri-rits bright, what fun it is to

laughing all the way. ride and sing a sleighing song to - night! Jingle bells, jing-le bells,

jingle all the way. Oh what fun it is to ride in a onehorse o-pen sleigh. Hey! onehorse o-pen

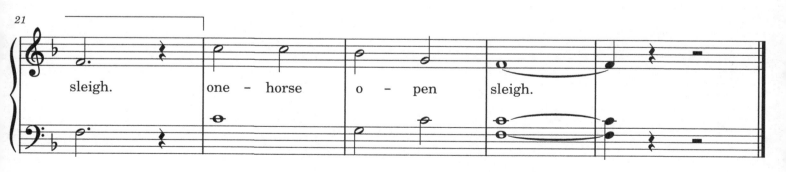

sleigh. one - horse o - pen sleigh.

JOLLY OLD SAINT NICHOLAS

♩ = 120 Happily

Jol - ly   old Saint   Ni - cho - las,   Lean your ear this   way!   Don't you tell a

single soul   What I'm goin to   say.   Christmas Eve is   coming soon;   Now you dear old   man,

Whis - per   what you'll   bring   to   me.   Tell   me   if   you   can.

JOY TO THE WORLD

Allegro

f Joy to the world, the Lord is come. Let earth re - ceive her King! Let ev - ery__ heart__ pre - pare__ Him__ room__ and heaven and na - tu - re sing, and heaven and na - tu - re sing. f And hea - ven, and hea - ven, and na - ture sing.

mf

LET IT SNOW!

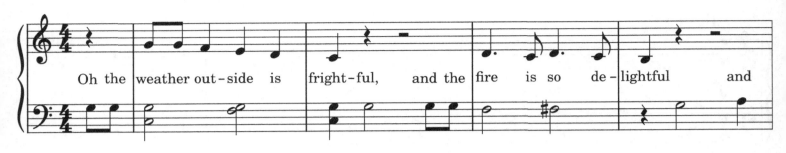

Oh the weather out-side is fright-ful, and the fire is so de-lightful and

since we've no place to go, let it snow, let it snow, let it snow! It doesn't show signs of

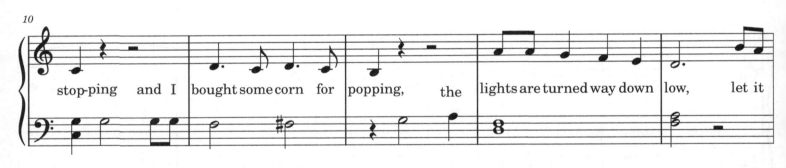

stop-ping and I bought some corn for popping, the lights are turned way down low, let it

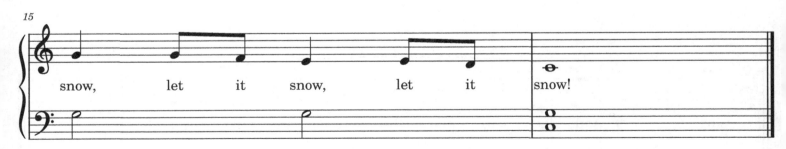

snow, let it snow, let it snow!

LITTLE DRUMMER BOY

"Come", they told me, pa - rampa pam - pam, _____ "our newborn King to see" pa -

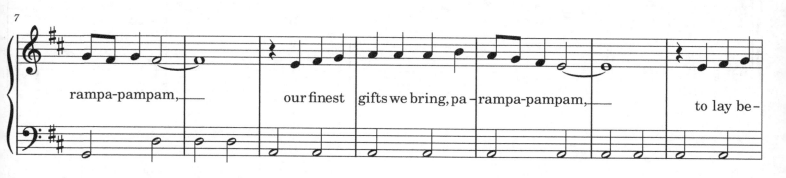

rampa-pampam, _____ our finest gifts we bring, pa - rampa-pampam, _____ to lay be-

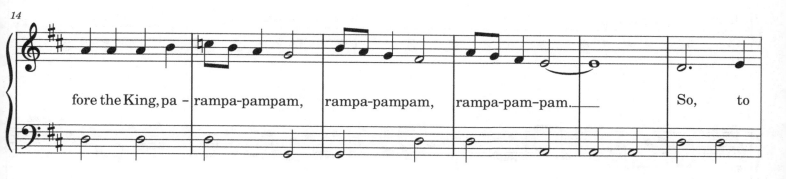

fore the King, pa - rampa-pampam, rampa-pampam, rampa-pam-pam. _____ So, to

hon - our him, pa - rampa pam - pam, _____ when we come. _____

MARCH FROM THE NUTCRACKER

MARY, DID YOU KNOW?

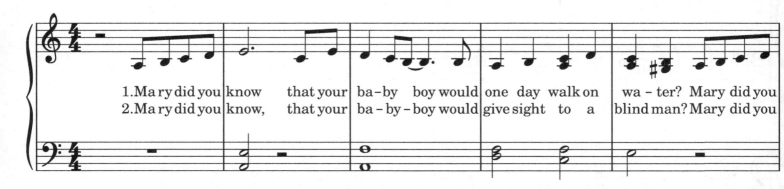

1. Ma-ry did you know   that your   ba-by boy would one day walk on   wa-ter? Mary did you
2. Ma-ry did you know,   that your   ba-by-boy would give sight to a   blind man? Mary did you

know   that your   ba-by-boy would save our sons and   daugh-ters? Did you   know - that your
know   that your   ba-by-boy will   calm the storm with His hand? Did you   know - that your

ba-by-boy has   come   to make you   new? This child that you - de - li - vered - would
ba-by-boy has   walked where an-gels trod? When you kiss your litt-le   ba-by - you

soon de-li-ver   you?   God? Mary did you know? The blind will see, the   deaf will hear, the
kissed the face of

50

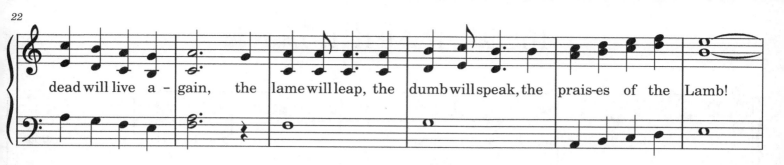

dead will live a - gain, the lame will leap, the dumb will speak, the prais-es of the Lamb!

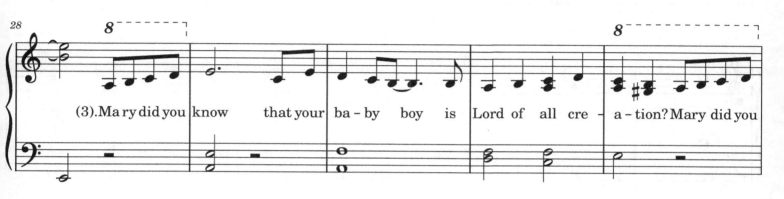

(3).Ma ry did you know that your ba - by boy is Lord of all cre - a - tion? Mary did you

know that your ba - by - boy will one day rule the nations? Did you know - that your ba - by - boy is

Heaven's perfect Lamb? The sleeping child you're hold-ing - is the great "I AM?"

MELE KALIKIMAKA

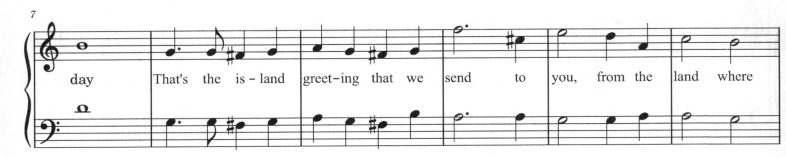

ma-ka is the thing to say, on a bright Ha-waii-an Christmas day

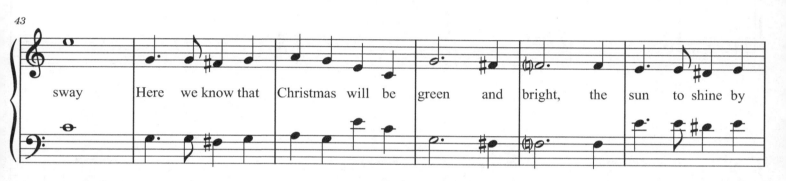

That's the is-land greet-ing that we send to you, from the land where palm trees

sway Here we know that Christmas will be green and bright, the sun to shine by

day and all the stars at night Me-le Ka-li-ki-ma-ka is Ha-wa-ii's way to say Me-rry

Christmas a ve-ry Me-rry Christmas a very very merrymerry Christmas to you

MERRY CHRISTMAS MR. LAWRENCE

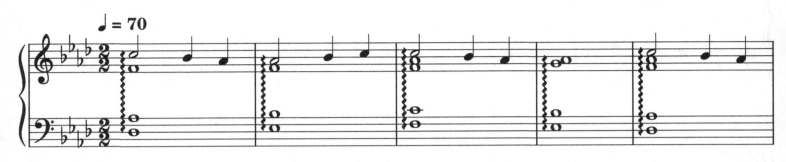

MY FAVORITE THINGS

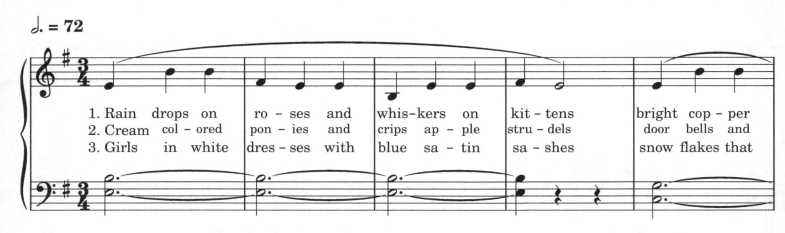

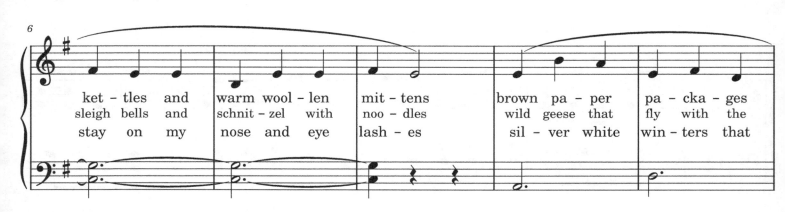

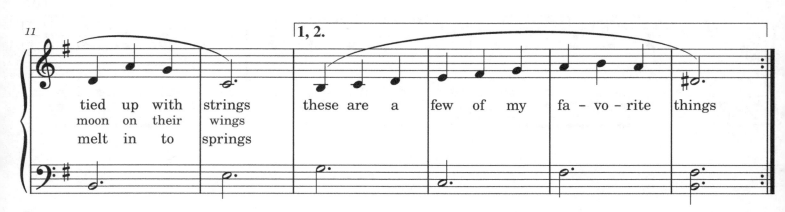

these are a few of my fa-vo-rite things   When the dog bites

when the bee stings   when I'm fee-ling sad   I

sim-ply re-mem-ber my fa-vor-ite things and then I don't feel

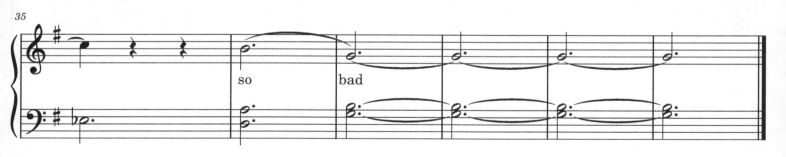

so   bad

O CHRISTMAS TREE

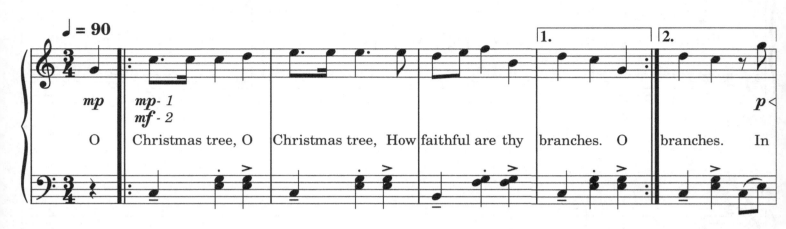

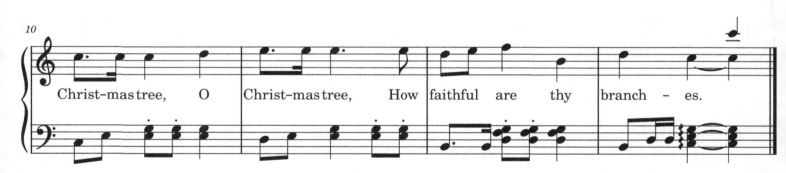

O COME, ALL YE FAITHFUL

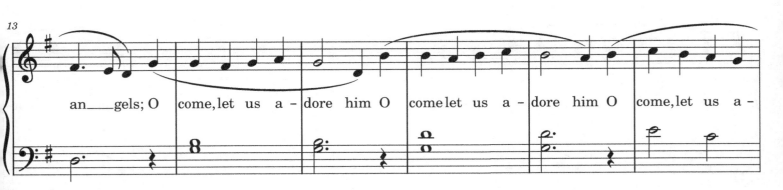

O COME, O COME EMMANUEL

O LITTLE TOWN OF BETHLEHEM

♩ = 85

1.O lit - tle town of Beth - le - hem, How still we see thee lie;
2.For Christ is born of Ma - ry; And gath - ered all a - bove,
3.How si - lent - ly, how si - lent - ly, The won - drous gift is giv'n!
4.O ho - ly child of Beth - le - hem, De - scend to us, we pray;

A - bove thy deep and dream - less sleep The Si - lent stars go by:
While mor - tals sleep, the an - gels keep Their watch of won - d'ring love.
So God im - parts to hu - man hearts The bless - ings of His heav'n.
Cast out our sin, and en - ter in, Be born in us to - day.

Yet in thy dark streets shin - eth The ev - er - last - ing Light;
O morn - ing stars, to - geth - er Pro - claim the ho - ly birth;
No ear may hear His com - ing, But in this world of sin,
We hear the Christ - mas an - gels The great glad tid - ings tell;

The hhopes and fears of all the years Are met in thee to - night.
And prais - es sing to God, the King, And peace to men on earth.
Where meek souls will re - ceive Him, still The dear Christ en - ters in.
O come to us, a - bide with us, Our Lord Em - man - u - el.

O HOLY NIGHT

Oh ho-ly night the

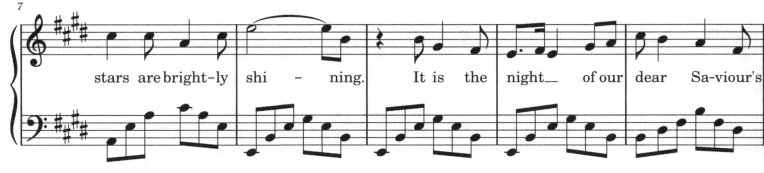

stars are bright-ly shi - ning. It is the night__ of our dear Sa-viour's

birth__ Long lay the world__ in sin and er - ror

pi - ning Till he ap - peared__ and the soul__ felt its

worth. oh - oh_____ A thrill of ho-pe the

wea - ry world re - joi - ces. For yon - der breaks a new and glo - rious

morn_____ Fall_____ on your knees_____ O

hear_____ the an - gels' voi - ces.____ O_____ night_____

_____ di - vi-ne_____ O_____ night_____ when Christ was

born._____ O_____ night_____ di - vi -

1.

ne holy night____ o night____ o night di - vi - ne.

PAT-A-PAN

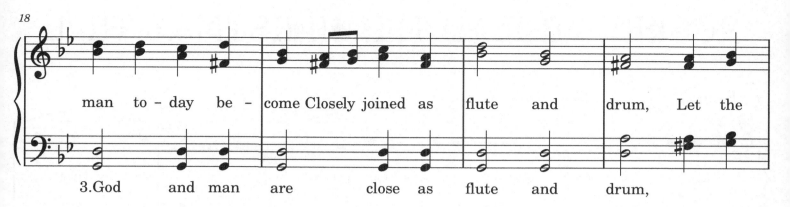

man to - day be - come Closely joined as flute and drum, Let the

3.God and man are close as flute and drum,

joy - ous tune play on! Tu - re - lu - re - lu, pat - a - pan - a - pan, As the

in - stru-ments you play, We will sing this Christ - mas Day.

ROCKIN' AROUND THE CHRISTMAS TREE

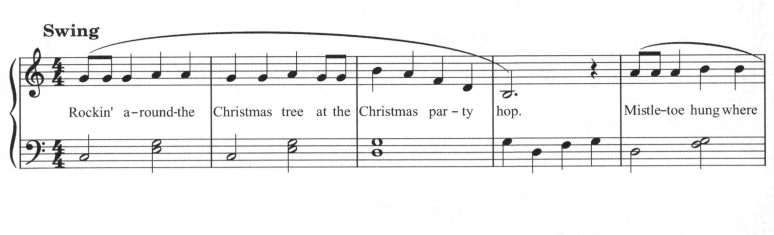

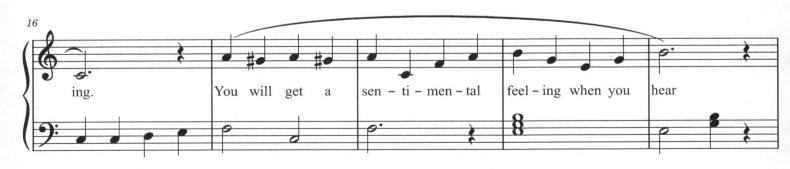

voic – es sing – ing "Let's be jol – ly, Deck the halls with boughs of hol – ly" Rockin' a – round the

Christ mas tree, have a hap – py hol – i – day Ev – 'ry – one danc – ing mer – ri – ly in the

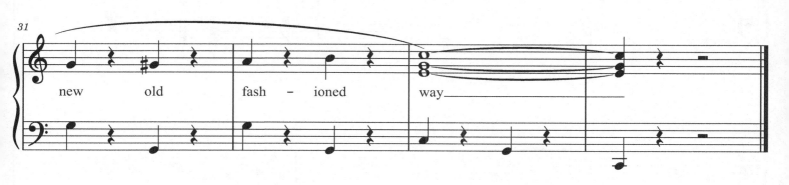

new old fash – ioned way

RUDOLPH THE RED-NOSED REINDEER

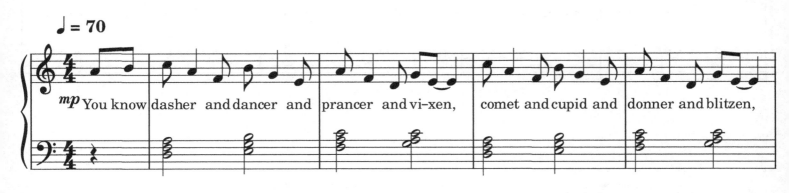

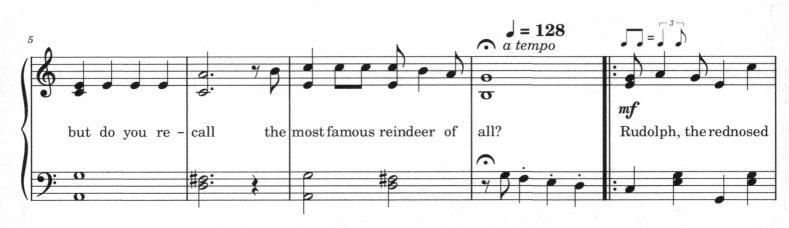

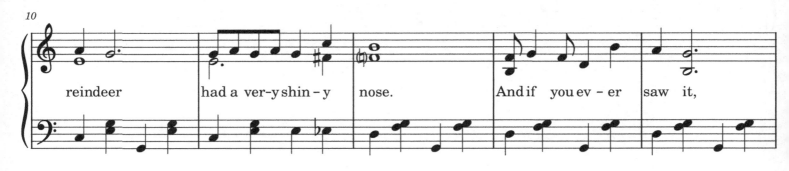

SANTA CLAUS IS COMING TO TOWN

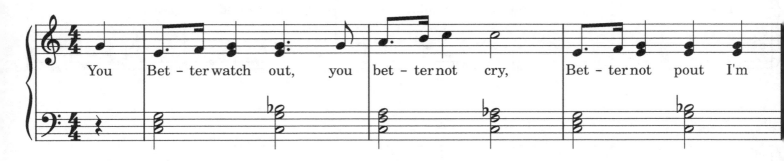

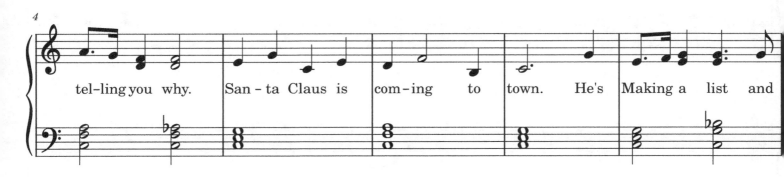

ake. He knows if you've been bad or good, so be good, for good-ness

sake. Oh, You Bet-ter watch out, you bet-ter not cry, Bet-ter not pout I'm

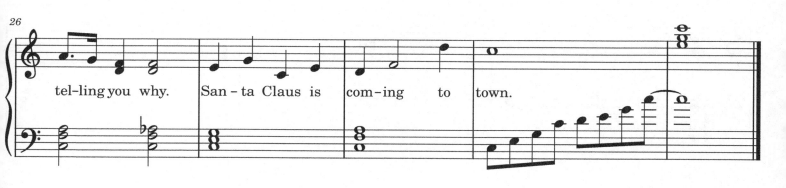

tel-ling you why. San-ta Claus is com-ing to town.

SILVER BELLS

Moderato

SILENT NIGHT

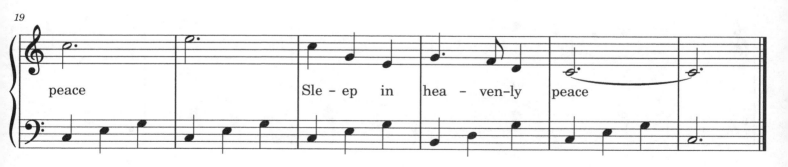

THE CHRISTMAS WALTZ

THE FIRST NOEL

WE THREE KINGS

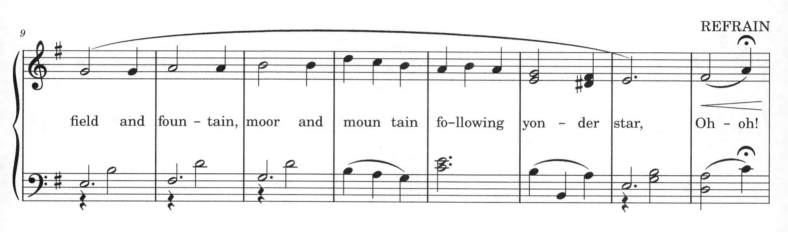

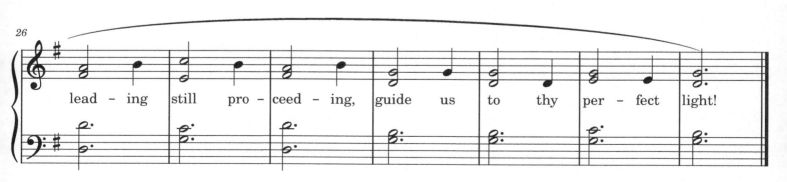

WE WISH YOU A MERRY CHRISTMAS

We | wish you a merry | Christmas, we | wish you a merry | Christmas, we | wish you a merry

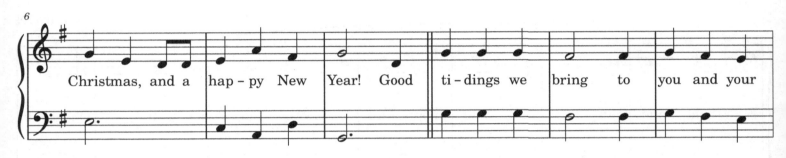

Christmas, and a | hap-py New | Year! Good | ti-dings we | bring to | you and your

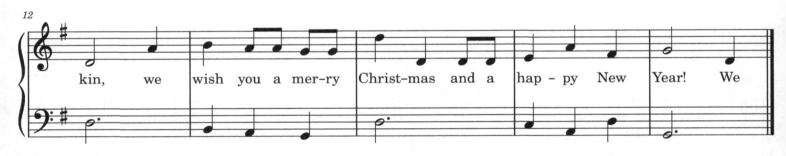

kin, | we | wish you a mer-ry | Christ-mas and a | hap-py New | Year! We

WHAT CHILD IS THIS?

What child is this who is laid to rest on Ma - ry's lap i - s

slee - ping Whom an - gels greet with ant - hems sweet while shep-herds wa-tch a-re

kee - ping This, this i - s Christ the King whom shep - herds guard an-d

ang - els sing Haste, ha-ste to bring him laud the babe the so - n of Ma - ry

WHITE CHRISTMAS

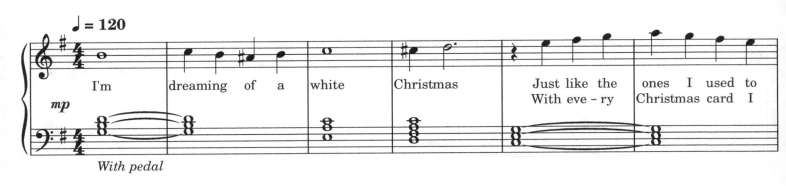

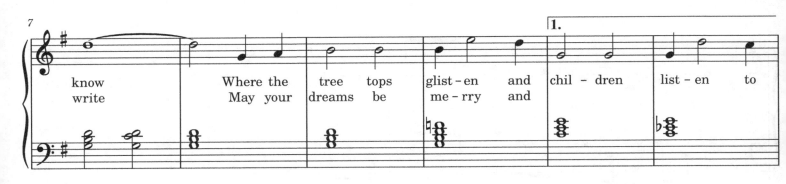

GET YOUR FREE BONUS PIANO BOOK!

Your Opinion Matters! Help Us Shape the Future of Piano Music

Dear Valued Customer,

We hope this message finds you well and that your musical journey continues to be a harmonious and fulfilling one. We wanted to reach out to you today to express our heartfelt gratitude for choosing our piano book «The Giant Book of CHRISTMAS SHEET MUSIC FOR PIANO», to be your companion on this melodious adventure.

As creators and musicians ourselves, we understand the pivotal role that feedback plays in refining and enhancing our craft. Your insights and opinions are invaluable to us, and we believe they have the power to shape the future of piano music. That's why we kindly request you to take a few moments out of your day to leave a review for «The Giant Book of CHRISTMAS SHEET MUSIC FOR PIANO».

Your review will not only help us understand what aspects of the book resonated with you the most but also guide us in making improvements to provide an even more enriching experience for aspiring pianists like yourself. By sharing your thoughts, you become an integral part of our creative process, and your contribution will be felt by countless others who embark on this musical journey.

Whether you found the exercises particularly helpful, the sheet music beautifully arranged, or the accompanying explanations insightful, your honest review will help fellow musicians make informed decisions. Your words could be the encouragement someone else needs to dive into the world of piano music and unlock their artistic potential.

Leaving a review is easy:

* Just scan QR Code with your phone and leave a good review if you like the book.

Thank you once again for choosing our book, and we eagerly await your insights. Together, we can create a harmonious and inspiring environment for every pianist to thrive.

May your music continue to resonate with passion and grace!

Warm regards,

Henry White

Made in the USA
Columbia, SC
24 December 2023

29420980R00050